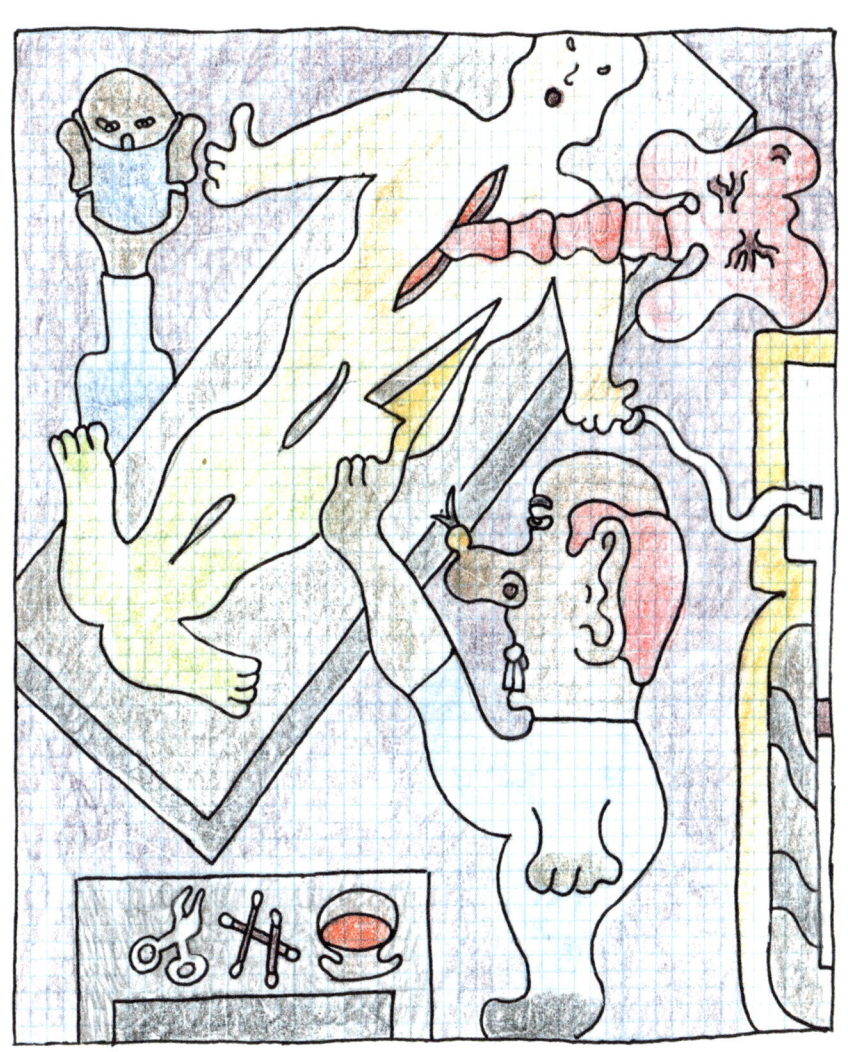

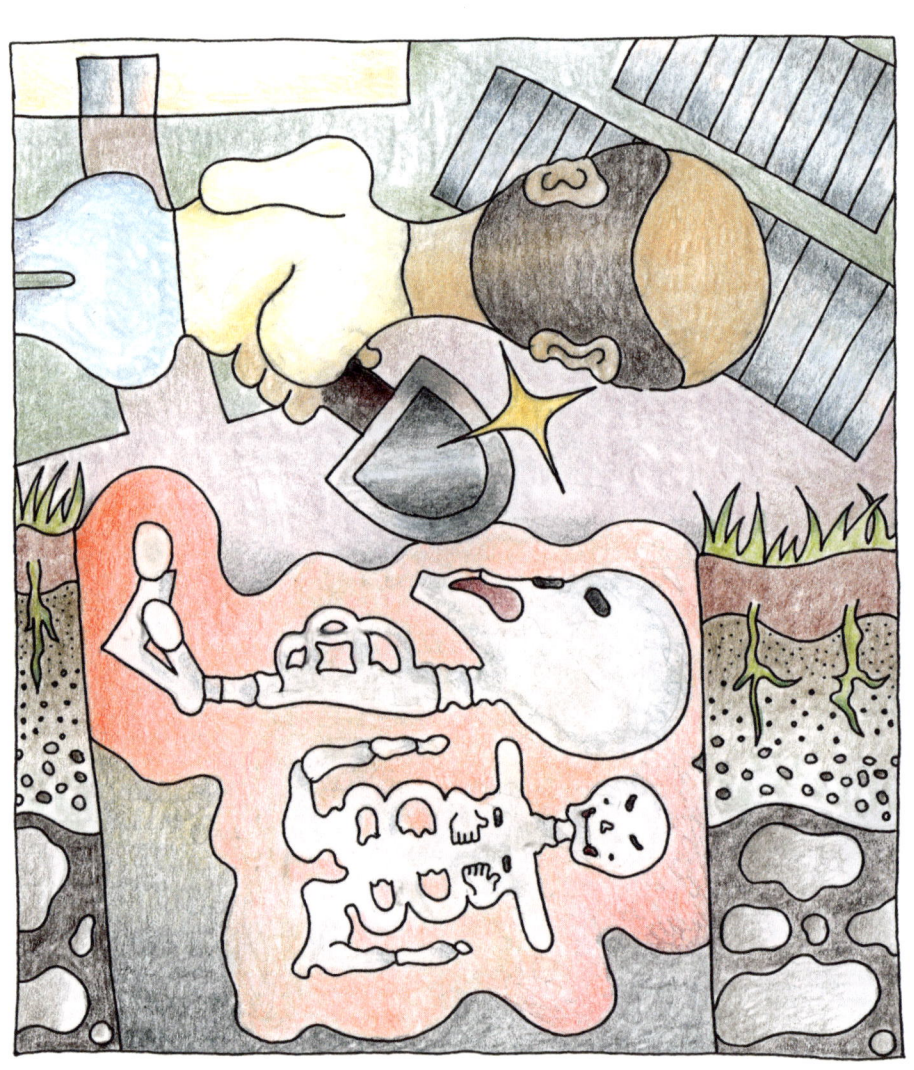

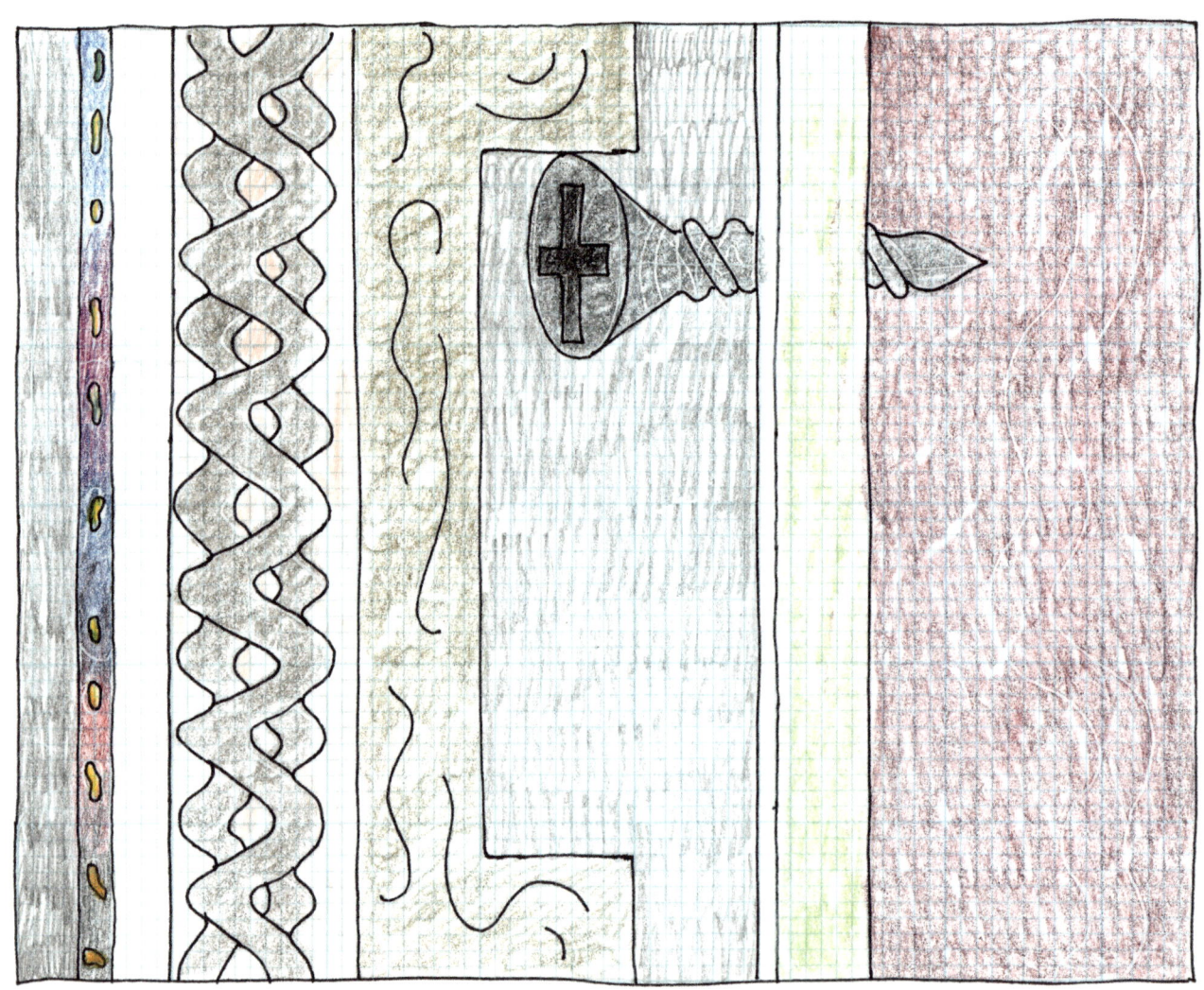

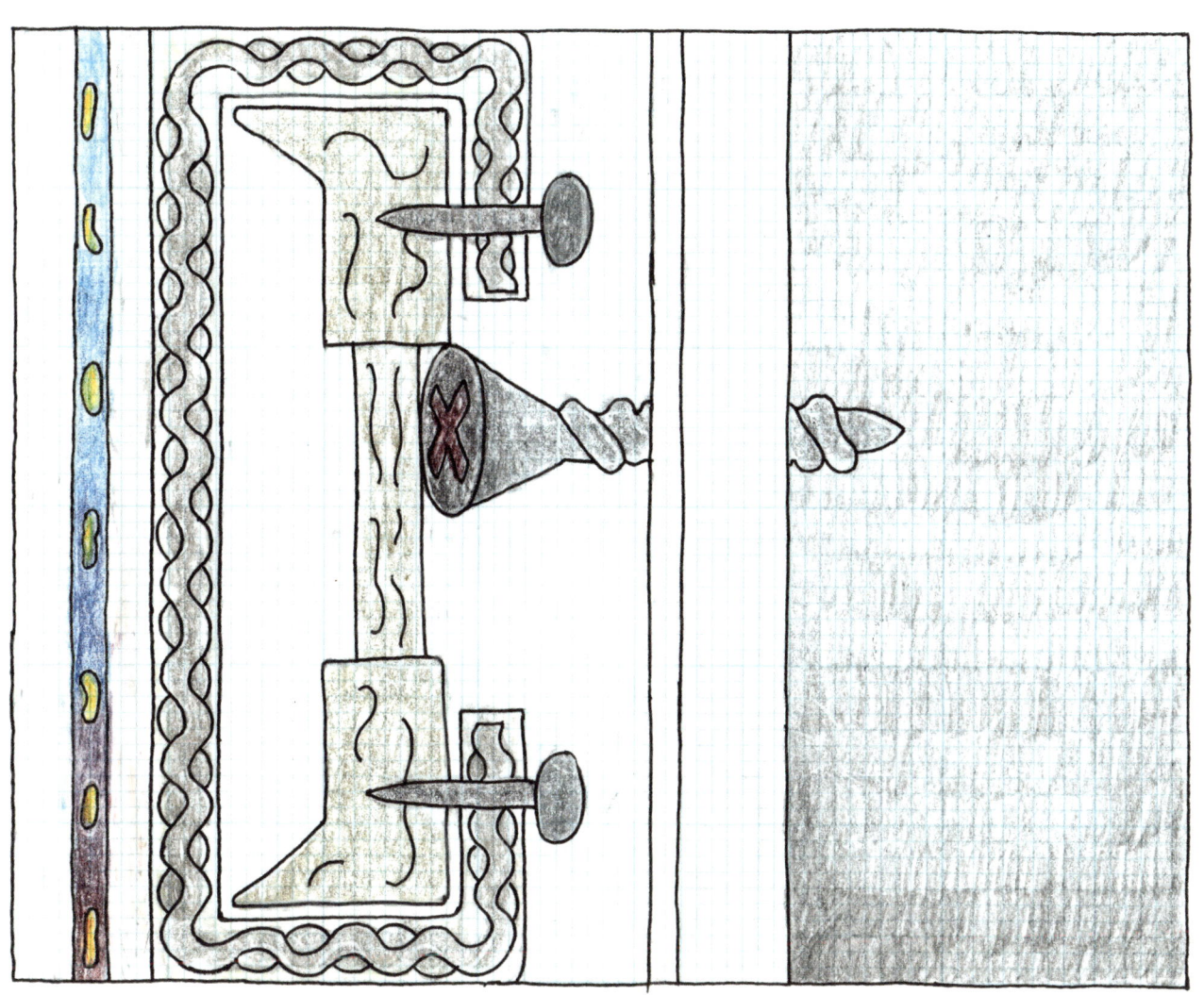

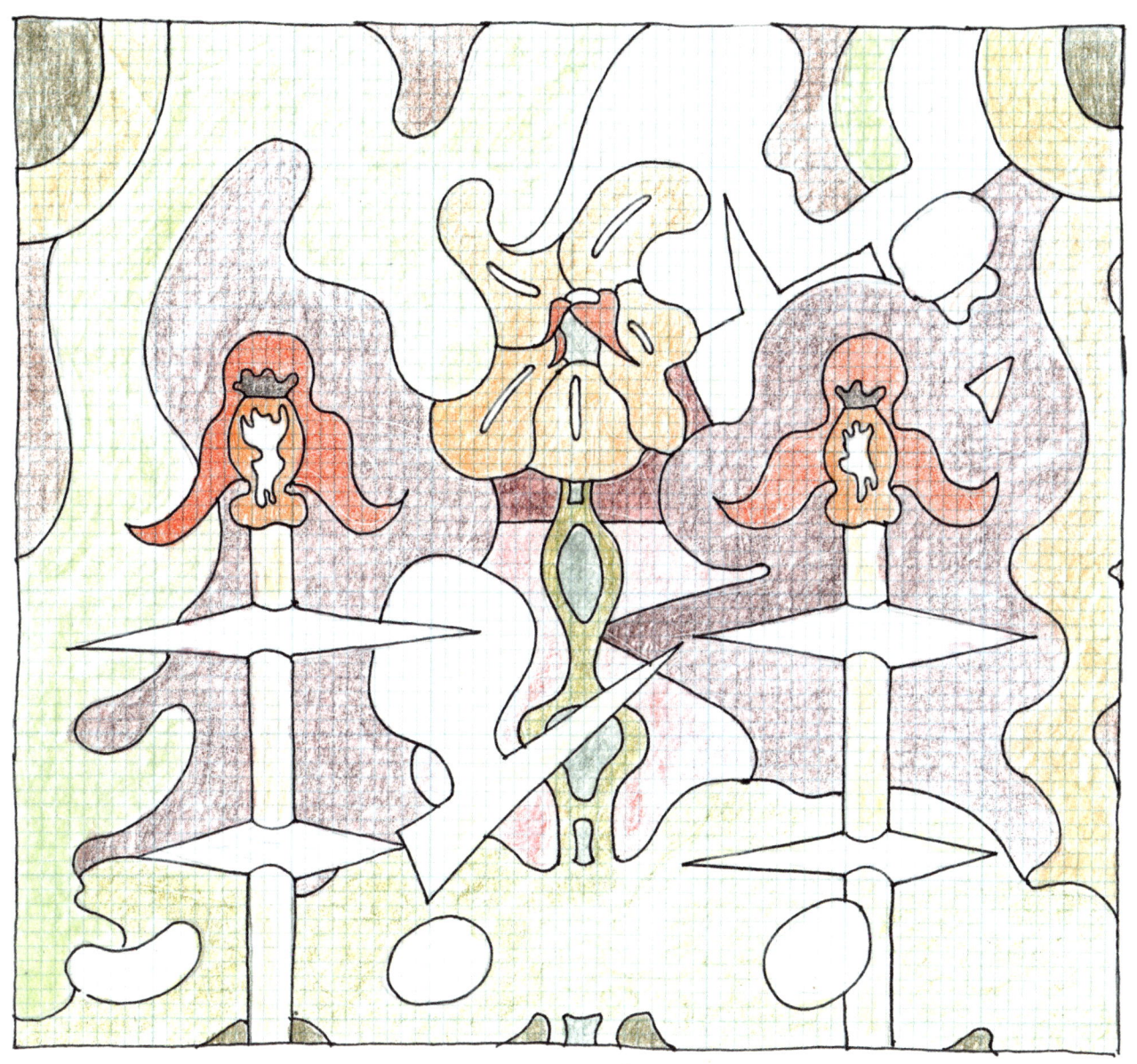

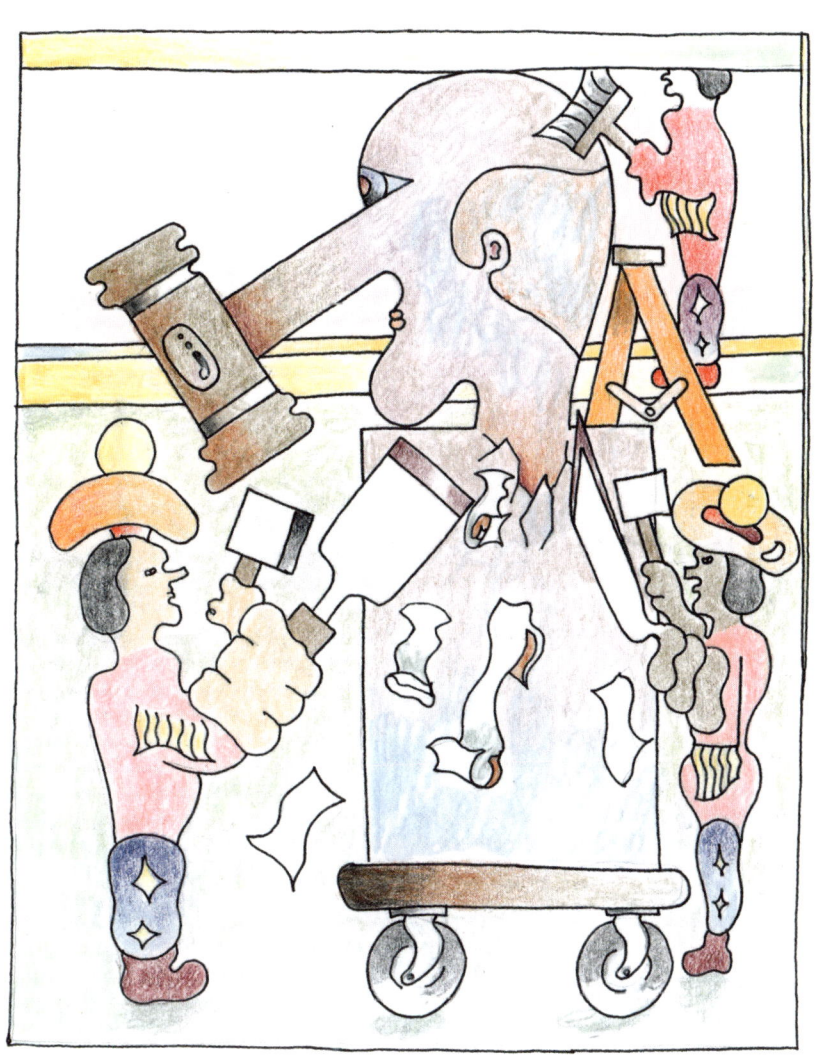

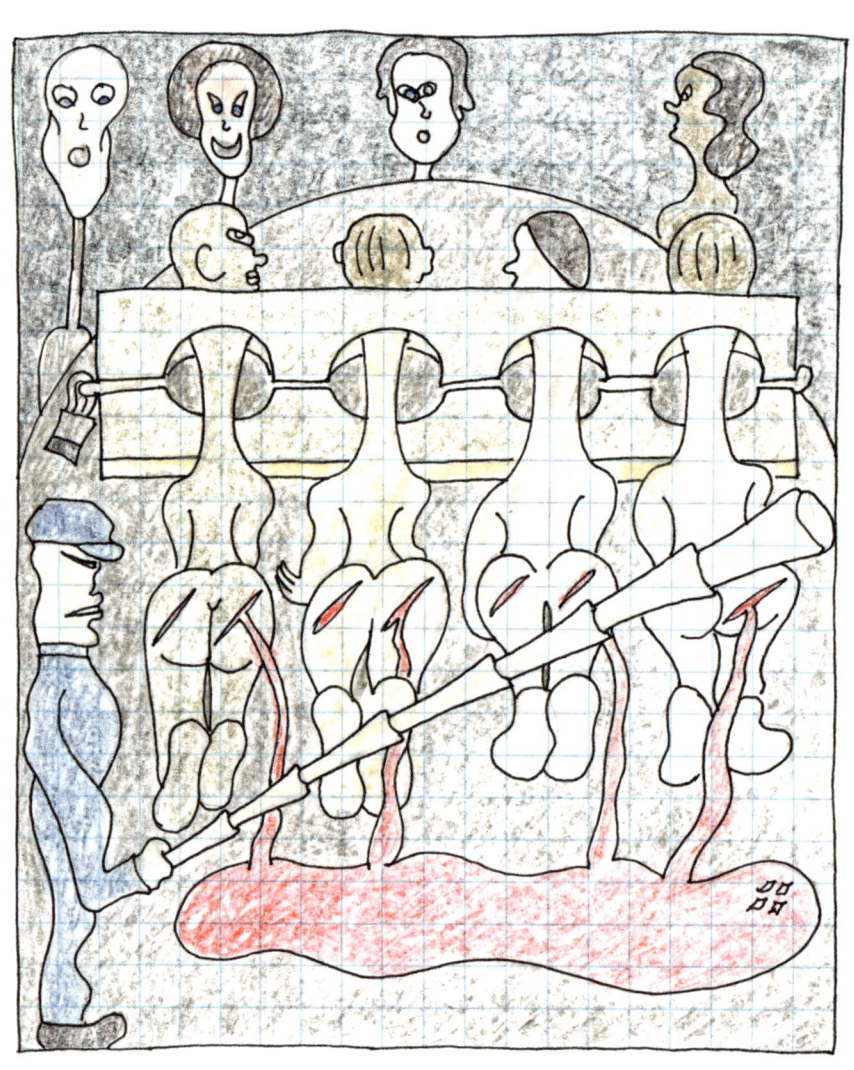

Keegan McHargue
Preparation K

First Edition

Published by Nieves
www.nievesbooks.com

Thanks to Joel, Alli & Max Sobaszek, and Carol Nhan

Copyright 2014 Keegan McHargue and Nieves
Reproduction without permission prohibited

ISBN 978-3-905999-54-9